THE LORD HAS SHOWN ME PEACE!

POEMS OF THE HEART!

PATRICIA OAKES IRVIN

Copyright © 2013 by Patricia Oakes Irvin

The Lord Has Shown Me Peace!
Poems Of The Heart!
by Patricia Oakes Irvin

Printed in the United States of America

ISBN 9781626978027

All rights reserved solely by the author. The author guarantees all contents are original and do not infringe upon the legal rights of any other person or work. No part of this book may be reproduced in any form without the permission of the author. The views expressed in this book are not necessarily those of the publisher.

Unless otherwise indicated, Bible quotations are taken from the King James Version of the Bible. Copyright © 2001 by G.E.M publishing.

www.xulonpress.com

Contents

The Lord Has Shown Me Peace! 4
Let Them Laugh! 6
Carry Me! 8
Passion! 9
Changing Seasons! .11
You Are Real! 12
AWAKE! 14
SILLY STARLING! 16
A Hug From Aunt Joyce! 18
Nathan's Smile! 19
Three A.M.! 21
Words! 22
Life's Choices! 24
Alone! 26
I Stand In Awe! 27
Refresh Me! 29
Grampa's Memory Swing! 30
His Mighty Plan! 31
A Changed Heart! 32
Never Hold Back! 34
Gramma's Kitchen With Love! 36
Lailah's Little Arms! 38
Without You Lord. .40

The Lord Has Shown Me Peace!

Because the Lord has shown me peace,
anger will not own my heart.
For when anger starts to show its face
I ask the Lord to take it on.
I ask in prayer, "Dear Lord , dear Lord
let forgiveness take its place."
I read His words and I am refreshed knowing
He does hear me, always.
Because the Lord has shown me peace I can rest
easy after praying in sincerity,
having faith that the Lord will answer in ways
that are best for me.
For me, I am of a foolish heart without Him,
and know not what is best.
Through prayer and study only can I come
close to understanding Him.

Because the Lord has shown me peace
I can enjoy the simplicity of life.
I can enjoy the light-hearted laughter of the
little children at play.
I can laugh at the silliness of the animals
as they scamper about so busily.
I can appreciate every day I get to see the sunrise,
and the sunset.

The Lord Has Shown Me Peace!

Because the Lord has shown me peace simple beauty
becomes so awesome.
The beauty of the changing seasons, the vibrant,
crisp colors of fall.
Oh, the beauty of winter snow-capped mountains and trees.
Spring, Spring, when flowers bloom, and the song birds
all return to sing.

Because the Lord has shown me peace,
His blessing become more clear.
His love is but so comforting, for He carries my
every worry and fear.
His strength, not mine has brought me through
so many battles in life,
and His love and peace that He has so graciously
shown will sustain me.

Let Them Laugh!

They laugh and point and say, "She's strange"
each day as she passes by.
Yet with a smile on her face she never fails
to wave and say hi.
And in return people point and laugh and
roll their eyes, but why?
For no harm she causes to deserve the
hatefulness people show.

And her penalty for showing kindness to everyone she sees,
daring to extend a wave to even those she doesn't know,
is a snicker and a roll of eyes, and a "Don't bother me".
I pass her almost daily and watch the snickering only grow.

Yet she still continues with a smile and a glimmer in her eye.
Why does she even bother? I just have to know.
So one day I stopped her and simply asked her why.
"Why do you even bother, when only hatefulness they show?"

"Because I choose to live a path less traveled,
the Lord's path of peace.
And they have chosen the path most traveled,
where anger is their guide.
And I simply will not let their anger swallow up my heart.
For I allow only the Lord to guide me, and
He is with me everywhere I go."

The Lord Has Shown Me Peace!

"I pray that as I do His will,

ignoring every snicker, every sigh,

that hearts will be made at peace and come to know,

the Lord our Savior's amazing love, is why.

For then His love and wisdom within their hearts will grow."

She turned to walk away, then quickly looked back at me,

and said, " I must ask you a question, if I may, before I go.

Why do you think it bothers you, the hatefulness you see?

For your heart must long to find that peace, is that not so?"

Carry Me!

Carry me Lord! For your mighty arms are as iron,
while my legs grow weary.
Lead me Lord! For your eyes are as many beacons,
guiding in every direction.
I am blind, and walk in darkness reaching out,
reaching out for your hand.
Let me hear your words so clear, for I am deaf,
and want to understand them.

Let me feel your love dear lord,
for my heart grows cold and weak,
and you, only you, can give my heart the warmth,
the strength it needs to heal.
For I know you heal the hearts, the hearts that truly
seek you in true faith.
Faith so deserving, for all your love, all your wonders,
many not yet known.

Carry me I pray dear Lord; without you I am as stone
without movement,
without heart, without mind, without feeling; carry
me, carry me.
You are my legs as I move, my heart as I feel,
my thoughts so I may reason.
In every way you carry me, in every way,
every waking day, I praise you.

Passion!

Her nose pressed against the store window and her eyes
widened with delight,
as the tiny ballerina on the music box dances around
with such grace.
This is the beginning of every day, her morning ritual
you might say.
A ritual that takes her cares away, for a moment,
as she twirls along her way.

How her heart dreams of one day dancing with such beauty
and such elegance.
Even for just a moment, every morn the little girl is
a graceful ballerina.
It takes a passion so intense, a burning desire,
to follow this daily ritual.
And not care who watches as her passion takes her
dancing along the way.

There is the little boy who leaves for school a bit
early every day.
To pass the neighborhood garage to stare at the mechanic
busy at his passion.
A passion so intense, a heart so yearning,
that even he doesn't understand it.
A single passion that this young heart shares,
and will probably one day follow.

The Lord Has Shown Me Peace!

Imagine if you will that their first, most burning passion
in their hearts,
Is that of knowing, and following our mighty Lord
and Savior's words.
Can you imagine the power, the beauty, the intensity
of their other passions?
With Christ's Holy Spirit, His love, His passion burning
first in their hearts.

We all have paths, we all have passions, let Christ be
your most burning desire.
Let His words echo in your ears, your heart be His,
His love overpower you.
Having faith in His promises to those who follow only Him.
With Christ as your first, most burning passion,
imagine the possibilities.

Changing Seasons!

Seasons change as surely as the sun will find its way,
through the darkest of clouds and noisiest of storms.
Then birds will sing in harmony, seems only for a day.
As the change of colors fill our eyes with beauty as it forms.

Then winter will be upon us, there is nothing we can say.
The snow will fall, and blanket all, the winter winds
will whine.
Then Spring will make its debut, bright flowers
with their aura,
will color our paths with beauty, leaving the cold behind.

Season after season will pass, but that's ok.
For they'll leave such vivid memories, pictures in our minds.
Children running in the snow on that cold December day.
Summer days spent swimming, oh how that sun did shine.

But the season most remembered was the spring you became mine.
To have and to hold forever, we did say.
No season will ever compare to that spring day my love.
For your love will forever take my breath away.

You Are Real!

When my heart feels like it holds a ton, and the weight is too much too bear.
When my heart is light with laughter and only joy I can feel.
I call on Him, I call on Him, I have no fear, He's always there.
Oh Lord; oh Lord; you bear my sorrows, you share my joys, you are real.

When my thoughts are filled with anger and they are less than clear.
When His words are my thoughts as I come before Him and kneel.
I call on Him, I call on Him, I have no fear, He's always there.
Oh Lord; Oh Lord; you bear my sorrows, you share my joys, you are real.

When this old body's pain is real and no one seems to care.
When I wake to sing a song and face life with such zeal.
I call on Him, I call on Him, I have no fear, He's always there.
Oh Lord; Oh Lord; you bear my sorrows, you share my joys, you are real.

I only know you'll give me strength, strength enough to bear.
Any wounds my heart will suffer, you will heal, for you are real.

I pray you help me understand your words, dear Lord; to share, all your wisdom and all your blessing. For dear Lord; you are so real.

AWAKE!

Here I am awake again with only my thoughts to carry me through the night.

Where they will take me I do not know, I'll just continue to write.

And let them take me where they may, I do hope they'll bring a smile.

So I can drift away in carefree thoughts that will stay with me awhile.

Or will my thoughts lead me astray to thoughts I need not think about?

Thoughts that only bring on tears, thoughts that make me want to shout?

I say, I say! Those thoughts can only put a cloud over the good things in my life.

Why should I waste my time on thoughts that will only bring on strife?

I choose to return to happy thoughts that have not clouds but only light.

And now I will continue to write, and smile, as I return to a happier site.

A site where I can drift away on only the happiest of times that make me smile.

And cherished thoughts that will help me close my eyes, and rest but for awhile.

The Lord Has Shown Me Peace!

We all have the choice of the thoughts that will clutter up our minds.

Will your thoughts be of darkness, or ones of cherished times?

I say choose your thoughts most carefully before they drift to a dark site.

Just remember the choice is yours, all yours. Good night!

SILLY STARLING!

Oh silly little starling, you silly little bird,
so tiny in this world.
To be so tiny in this world you surely let your
presence be heard.
I heard you even from the nest long before my eyes took sight,
And long before your mamma coaxed you into taking
your first flight.

Still up there in my tree, all alone making such a fright.
When the rest of your family has flown away you remain,
such a sight.
Even though it brings me laughter to watch you,
you silly little bird.
And distracts me but for a moment, and lightens
my heavy heart,

I know you cannot stay. So go, my little friend,
go find your way.
Mamma taught you well, she prepared you for your survival.
So that one day you would, and could leave to venture out.
Venture out to make your own nest in someone else's tree.

So fly away my silly friend for your mamma taught you well.
Go! Bring someone else smiles with your silly
light-hearted ways.

The Lord Has Shown Me Peace!

And distract them from their troubles,

even if just for a single moment.

And with you in all your travels my little friend,

the Lord is sure to be.

A Hug From Aunt Joyce!

When you feel one of her hugs you know you are really,
truly loved.
For in her warm hugs she gives all the love she has, and more.
You do not walk in her door without receiving one,
nor leave without one.
A hug that would have to last until our next family gathering.

When you see her smile you see pure happiness and pure joy.
For it gives her warm heart such happiness
and joy just to see us.
I only pray she knows how much she means to
every heart she touches.
And in case she doesn't know by now how much,
I am telling her.

I speak for everyone she has touched, and every heart
that she opened.
And everyone who has felt her hugs, and everyone who
has seen her smile.
You are a precious blessing in each and everyone of our lives
May the Lord put His arms around you to show
how much you're loved.

Nathan's Smile!

He captures the hearts of many instantaneously
with his charming smile.
For through his boyish smile his tender heart
becomes transparent.
A young heart so willing to be open, so willing to give,
so willing to share.
May his heart always stay open, and be in the
Lord's tender care.

His eyes so sparkle as he greets you, his arms wide open
with such delight.
A heart that does not know a stranger; everyone,
anyone is welcome in.
Just one time meeting our Nathan is all it takes, then
you will see.
That loving him comes all so easy, I dare any heart,
any heart resist.

In eight short years he has brought many smiles,
and many tears.
But every smile and tear were ones of love that we all share.
For our one and only Nathan, a gift the Lord has sent our way.
He's all boy, all heart, all giving,
there is not much more to say.

Except to him, and that is, "Nathan never doubt how much you're loved.

And never doubt that you are a gift the Lord has brought into our lives.

I will pray each day that as you grow and make your way in this big world

that you will love the Lord, and understand His deep, amazing love for you."

Three A.M.!

It's three A.M. early morn and I can't turn this
clock off in my head.
The dog just lies there blankly staring, wondering,
"Why is she not in bed?"
A question I have asked myself so many times,
but it still remains a mystery.
She should be so used to this, the dog that is.
We've been here before, you see.

Just her and I and my keyboard while everyone else
is still in bed.
It's funny though how at times like this, with little
being said.
When everyone else is fast asleep and it's as quiet
as it can be,
that I get the most accomplished. For then,
my mind just wanders free.

So then maybe there's a reason this clock goes off
inside my head,
and goes off so early in the morn to get me out of my warm bed.
For it seems this old wandering mind works best at three
A.M., you see.
Well, well what do you know, I've solved a mystery.

Words!

Choose your words most carefully,

are they what you mean to say?

For some words can hurt for life and will always

get in the way.

And will forever ring in the ears of the ones

that you most cherish.

Because your words go straight to their heart

they tend to never perish.

We seem to take the time to carefully choose the words

we want to say.

With ones we hardly know, people we pass along the way.

But yet to the ones we love the most we'll utter words

we will regret.

And to them they are the most hurtful and harder to forget.

Do not the ones we love the most, ones we carry in our heart,

deserve the careful choosing of our words,

and caring how we part?

For have they not held you in their heart,

and given love so endlessly?

And when your heart needs comfort are they the ones

you want to see?

Just stop! Take a minute, and put careful thought

in what you say.

Are they only words of anger that will turn a heart away,
and do such hurtful damage that you did not mean to do?
Last but not least, are they words you would want said to you?

Life's Choices!

Life will bring you many choices, and life-changing
some will be.
Many will not be easy, in fact some challenging at best.
There will be some that will make you feel like
you must act in haste.
But stop! Have patience. Do not be hastened
by an unclear mind.

Let the Lord be your first and most important choice
as these challenges arise.
Let Him battle with the choices that burden your heart,
for you cannot.
Put them in His care where confusion does not, cannot rest.
He can clear the unclear mind and ease the heart
that He knows best.

Not another soul could aid you in these challenges
you will face.
His power and love for us overwhelming, so hard for
us to grasp.
He has the power to make our choices for us, but He will not.
For His choice is for us to come to Him
our Lord most willingly.

Again! Life is filled with choices,
but by far the most important one,

Is to choose to live a life with the Lord's

bright light to shine your way.

A light to lead you from the darkness in this world,

that can lead you astray.

So let His light of truth be your guide

in your choices every day.

Alone!

How sad it is, how sad it is, the man who needs no one.
The man who always stands alone will surely one day see,
That alone is what he'll be when each day is done.
"I do not need others to clutter up my life, let me be,
let me be;"

Standing in a darkness all alone, when there could be sun.
For God the Father says to him who is alone, "Woe is he.
He'll have not another to pick him up when he falls, no one.
For people will tire of trying and alone they will
let him be."

Walk in darkness no more, open up your heart, even just to one
The one and only amazing Lord, He will not forsake thee.
He will fill your heart with all you need, so do not walk
to Him but run.
And you will long to share your heart,
never alone again to be.

Ecclesiastes 4:9-10

I Stand In Awe!

As I lie here on a night so bright with stars taking
over the sky,
the brilliance of your handiwork is so clear my dear,
dear Father.
You have given us such beauty. With our eyes we see
the beauty of the ocean,
and the song birds, to wake us every morning
with their cheery tune.

The sun You gave to guide our paths so safely through the day.
The moon to be our evening light as we end each blessed
and wondrous day.
Even the rain has its beauty showering us with flowers
after the storm.
The sun's warmth is but a blessing as it brings the flowers
to full bloom.

To the smallest of creatures you have given protection
from their predators.
The birds with their nest, the fox with its hole,
even the tiny turtle with its shell.
To keep us safe, dear Father, you put us in the care
of such mighty hands;
in the hands of our Lord and Savior to guard us
from our predator, the evil one.

Yet many in their arrogance refuse to turn to the
Lord's arms of safety.
For the evil one, he lurks to devour the many
arrogant hearts unguarded,
to plant his evil thoughts, and we say man is the
wisest of all creation.
To surrender to your will for us through Jesus Christ your
son, is most wise.

For one day all will understand your will,
and your love for man.
That your will, not through arrogance but through love for us,
will be done.
That Christ in all His glory will take full command as you,
Father, intended.
And the beauty of His Kingdom He will share with
those who follow Him.

Refresh Me!

Refresh me Lord with your words as sparkling water
from a spring.
Please ! Let them satisfy my thirst and help me to understand.
I thirst so for your words, in my ears let them ring,
let them ring.
As only you can do my dear Lord, yes! Only You can.

Refresh my heart with your love like no other soul
could bring.
Heal each scar of my wounded heart with your own loving hands.
I long to feel your joy, I long for my heart to sing.
As only you can do my dear Lord, yes! Only You can.

Refresh my soul, I pray, with a peace You alone can bring.
Let your wisdom be my guide and my strength,
help me firmly stand.
Let me speak your words so clearly to let all know you're King
As only you can do my dear Lord, yes ! Only You can.

Refresh my thoughts, let my worries fly away on eagles' wings.
Let your thoughts be mine, let me be at your
righteous command.
For I want to be there on that day; all know you are our
mighty King.
As only you can do my dear Lord, yes! Only You can.

Grampa's Memory Swing!

The stories he would tell as we sat upon his swing.
His most treasured memories, stories of his youth.
With eyes so wide with wonder, oh the laughter
they would bring.
He made his childhood come alive for us, before our very eyes.

His fascinating childhood seemed hard for us to grasp.
As he added twists to every story, leaving questions
for us to ask.
Then with hours of contentment, we sang songs he used to sing.
Even he was quite surprised to find he remembered every word.

As I sit here drowned in my memories on this old wooden swing,
and try to recall the words of the songs he used to sing.
I can hear his gentle voice, and feel his stroke upon my head.
Remembering all the love he put into every tale he said.

His Mighty Plan!

God created all things for good; He had a plan you see.

To make us in His image to please Him, the Almighty.

His plan included beauty, that would bring us to our knees.

But we need only to follow Him, for His love holds the key.

That is why He sent His son to give us a chance at peace.

But man ridiculed and mocked Him, and that's to say the least.

He traveled many miles with His words of truth to teach.

Man did not want the truth, so they laughed at Jesus's speech.

And yet now we still deny Him, our Savior; how can that be?

Man would tire of the hatefulness and pain, it seems to me.

Let Jesus own you heart and soul, and let Him oversee.

That was, still is our Father's plan,

and now Jesus holds the key.

A Changed Heart!

As I drift into my own little world of frustration,
at the end of a busy day.
A day of being mommy, now, watching my children
at the park as they play.
with their screeches, and their laughter,
"Mommy watch us", they would say .
While I grow impatient for some quiet time,
and I turn to look away.

My eyes behold a sight of beauty that stops my heart,
and clears my thoughts.
A young mother passes by strolling her young child
that's bound to a chair.
She smiles, even laughing, as her other little one
runs to play.
Not meaning to stare but almost uncontrollable,
I watch them with amazement.

Such spirit they all have, as the mother pushes
a younger sibling on a swing.
Playing, and not a single complaint they utter just
lots of love and laughter.
Suddenly my world turns from frustration to one of many,
many blessings.
Forever will I keep the picture of this family
and their loving spirits

The Lord Has Shown Me Peace!

As my attention turns back to watch my two little blessings

busy at their play.

I realize on days when we get overwhelmed and

negativity gets in the way.

The Lord can bring us to our knees in prayer and

thankful for each day,

and can instantaneously change a heart without Him

having much to say.

Never Hold Back!

Cradle them for as long as they will allow,

for such time passes quickly.

For all too soon they will struggle for their

independence and venture out.

Flying from your arms of safety and warmth into a

world of uncertainty.

Remember! A child is a child and will do foolish things

while finding their way.

Even when their independence seems to pull them away,

never hold back.

Keep your heart wide open, show your love for them

to be ever secure.

Give to them your time, your precious time without limit,

without measure.

Your open heart and precious time will transcend

through the years.

Until she is no longer a child, but now has a mother's heart,

And he now a man putting his foolish ways behind him.

As you hear your own words of caution uttered

from their mouths,

to their children they love dearly,

with every fiber of their being.

You will know your love was so instilled that it

carried on and on.

And your words that seemed to be unheard did

transcend the years.

For perfection was not in you but you never did hold back

your open heart, your precious time,

your love for them so clear.

Gramma's Kitchen With Love!

The wonderful smells that woke us on an early Sunday morn.
As we rubbed our sleepy eyes not caring,
that it was barely dawn.
Jumping out of bed, running down the stairs,
"Hurry, Hurry," we would say.
All racing to follow where those wonderful smells would lead.
To Gramma's kitchen, for we all knew, it came as no surprise.

For those wonderful smells that woke us was Gramma's
breakfast feast.
"No feast before my morning hugs", she'd say,
smiling all the while.
We'd race to the sink to wash our hands,
before we did partake.

Her breakfast feast was scrumptious, but more dear
to our hearts,
was her time she gave and the love she put into all she did.
How priceless were those weekend visits and
the memories they made.
For in our hearts her smile will be, never will it fade.

As I return to her kitchen that brought so much love and
start to reminisce,
A sight brings a happy tear to these wandering eyes.

The Lord Has Shown Me Peace!

There beside her apron is her favorite skillet,

both hanging on the wall.

When I realize the blessing she was to our lives,

my tear turns to a smile.

Lailah's Little Arms!

She stands there with her arms stretched out waiting
to be filled with hugs.
And big brown eyes filled with love so real, so sincere, and
meant for you.
What could be more of a blessing than to have the love
of this little heart?
One of our Lord's many blessings that I could not imagine
missing out on.

Her little girl giggles that say, "I am just happy
you came to play with me."
Then with rubbing of her eyes, it's nap time ,
and on my lap she rests.
As she lies there so peaceful, so still, I wonder
what her future might be.
Then I ask the Lord to direct her in the way that
only He knows best.

My dear little Lailah with your arms reaching out
with so much love,
and your eyes, they sparkle as diamonds with
every single silly smile.
There are so many who love you, I know, for I am
high up on that list.
But at the very top of that list is a love so mighty,
pure, and so true.

The Lord Has Shown Me Peace!

For at the very top of the list of all the hearts
you have won,
Is our Lord Jesus Christ In whose arms I know you're
sure to be safe.
So my dear little Lailah as you rest peacefully in my arms,
I ask the Lord to comfort you, and keep you safe,
as no one else can

Without You Lord

I am of a simple mind without you Lord, without wisdom,
without reason.
My heart is of stone without you Lord, without feeling,
without compassion.
I am weak without you Lord, so weak, as weak as the thinnest
of two twigs.
I see only darkness without you Lord, stumbling as I try
to find my way.

With your wisdom man's foolishness becomes clear,
as such, foolishness.
With your heart I can love without condition,
forgive seven times seventy.
With your strength this broken body of mine can do
unimaginable works.
Let me not be arrogant and take credit for your wonders,
yes your wonders.

Being an instrument of your righteousness may I show
your love, your truth,
So I can inspire ones who are so lost, and comfort ones
who are in need.
And I always come to you in prayer to be my counselor,
and my mighty guide.
May I be content to claim your blessings, and bring glory
to your holy name.

www.ingramcontent.com/pod-product-compliance
Lightning Source LLC
LaVergne TN
LVHW081526060526
838200LV00044B/2012